My Heart and Her Eclipse

Amy Anna

My Heart and Her Eclipse

ISBN: 978-1-914275-97-5

Perspective Press Global Ltd

Letter to my first love

The first boy to hold my heart in his hands should have been kind. He should have tasted like starry night skies and flowing forest water. Instead, he tasted of copper blood and regret.

First love, you took everything. You left my soul a cemetery: 'Happiness lies here', 'Laughter lies here' & 'Hope lies here'. Everything that ever lay within me, lies here. You took it all out of spite and left. I kept hoping maybe one day you'll just float away but I've realized the memory of you won't ever float away while it's chained to me. I was in the arms of a love that craved to see the sting of an open wound.

I could never find the words to describe the rabbit hole I was down in. It was my loneliest moment and darkest hour. Even as a writer, there's not a story nor poem I could write that could ever give me a sense of healing from the way I experienced his love. Fear is ultimately everything, it was the seed, and it was the water. He would tighten his grip around my voice box and taunted me to scream, he knew no one could hear - that power was his feed.

First love, what hurt the most was when you pretended to love me. You told me I was unlovable, you told me that for the past three months you felt nothing for me. Yet you continued to drain every ounce of happiness and life out of me, until you added mine to your 'jar of hearts.' Part of me still yearns for the apology I was told I never deserved.

Writing was my safe haven; it gave me a healthy sense of progression. I kept telling myself 'little poet you will write' but you will also ache. There are poems inside of your heart that the pages of your bestseller can't yet quite comprehend but first you must let it shatter to set them free. No one will write the way you do; no other woman's poetry will twist his tongue in the same clasps as yours did. She will sing him songs that will leave him empty for her rhymes will never fulfil him in the way that yours did. He will fill his bed with brunettes who taste like passion fruit, but they will never feel like home. Her laugh will never gut punch him in the ways yours does - oh how he pleads to hear it again just one more time. 'Little poet you are more woman than he will ever be man.'

First love, the last day I saw you is a blur to me. I remember the faint taste of coffee on my lips and how you wanted to kiss them on your way out the door. I didn't let you - it was your last hour, and my first to never crumble into your hands again. Your parents filed for divorce that day - a week prior, your father had trapped your mother after a disagreement, he held her under his thumb and called her weak. She was a strong but naïve woman. I wanted to be nothing like her - I pitied her. I refused to let you warp me in the web of abuse your parents let sleep within their marriage years ago.

Seven months later we met again, I saw it in your eyes that day, or maybe I heard it within your laugh. A glimpse or perhaps flashback of what made me fall in love with you. It's like bait in a mouse trap, it is sweet, and it is kind until it leaves you bruised and gasping for air. To one minute, see your eyes light a thousand cities and the next burn down poetry in forests. Or even one minute remember how it felt to lay my head on the pads of your shoulder

and feel your nails break the flesh of my wrists as you slur vulgar words through gritted teeth in the next.
Lying was like breathing to you, manipulation was your best friend. I was given no warning and I was lured in - heart first. You played me like a violin for your own amusement, pulling at the strings to watch them snap beneath your fingertips; nothing gave you greater pleasure than that. Nothing gave you greater pleasure than objectifying a young girl's heart and body that did not belong to you.

'This is not living'
I wept on my knees in the arms of the evening sun.
'I know'
she whispers running her fingers through the rustles within my hair.
'But I will rise again and so will you.'
-I always do

Autumn

Autumn kissed the tips of my toes as I stepped foot in the dewy courtyard, she blew strands of my hair off my cheeks and held me in her embrace.
She told me she was sorry for my hurt and promised to keep me safe.

Where there was love there was life.
Where there was once a smile that was adored there is an absence that left behind a million broken hearts.

A Writer

My fingertips burned as I eagerly ran them past each page of the rustled newspaper.
Searching for the answer that I planted within those very sheets many months back.
Growing up as a girl I was always taught to never speak with my mouth full.
For every time a man would shove the word 'hush' between my lips, I learned to remain quiet.
Writing for me was a form of escapism, one that my partner refused to understand.
I'll never forget the first time he placed my hands on his lap and asked me about all the dangerous things I love to do.
He asked me what made the morning sun kinder to wake up to - I told him I write.
He took a sharp breath and stiffened his neck. 'Will that pay the bills?' he questioned.
'Most likely not' I replied. I'd love it to though. I wish those starry night skies spent writing perched up on windowsills would pay all the bills.
I wish these words would fall from my heart into the lap of a couple million.
I wish I could pour myself into the arms of verses read from the pages of a bestseller.
I wish that one day my words would run rivers and start fires or have my poetry make people fall in love in the deepest ways possible.

My Partner was awfully fond of challenging me.
'You're not being practical!'
He'd hurl, expecting me to crumble at the abuse in his words.
'I wasn't trying to be practical I was trying to be brave' and with every attempt he made, he succeeded.
I should have known something that won't pay the bills won't ever fulfil him.

Butterfly kisses left on freckled noses in the grains of sand
a summer or two ago, I still have never loved you more.
I left the beach that day with the smell of the shore on the
sleeves of my cardigan, its pockets full of the laughter we
sang on the ridges of the dunes.
-It was one of the happiest days of my life

I smell you between the pages of the books that water my heart.
-The love that mattered most

Woman

While the sun kisses the pedals of June summer has just rolled on in.
It's been a year and still I sometimes feel lonelier than ever.
I heavily question the woman I've become and if I would've been a better one had I never known you at all.
You devoured parts of my femininity from a very young age that I can never take back.
To hold the innocence of a girl's first love within your grasp and groom it still, is a callous thing to do.
There are nights I lie awake and wonder if I'm whole, if I am a lost cause, if I'm not too far gone.
I would scrape pieces of myself off the tiled bathroom floor from the beatings I took on days you decided I was not good enough.
The girl who sobbed in the frosted mirror trembled and she quivered. I've never seen such a scarier sight than her.

I hope you experience this love

I hope you drain that boy.
I hope the lack of your love leaves his tongue aching.
I hope he loves you recklessly his knees scrape and his hands blister, yet he still begs for more.
I hope you leave him chasing, his lungs pumping, tired and sore.
I hope he makes you feel light and important, like you are one of the universe's most valuable treasures.
I hope he looks at you like you are the birth of a new sunrise, always.
I hope you tease, drag and lead.
And finally, I hope he asks to do it all over again.

Stale cups of coffee sit purposelessly on your bedside locker.
Your carpet has been clotting with dust you haven't brushed for weeks.
This sight is all too familiar.
There is too much going on up there, in that head of yours.
that nothing is happening here, where you stand.
-it is all part of the process

Seasonal

It's gotten colder now. The fog lays itself upon the dewy grass on mornings – the same grass where I feel at my loneliest. Something about September breaks me.
The warmth of the coffee cup tingles in my palms, my breath is the only sign of life when it meets the bitter air.
Although it is lonely it feels somewhat safe.
I am aware of the inevitable but as soon as October falls in I have no strength to keep going. October is kind. She knows how heavy my heart is and how at a loss my soul can be.
I know it pains her for there's nothing she can do about it. September left bruises just below my left lung so half of me
still
struggles
to
breathe.

His eyes are an earthy green, the kind of eyes that give your heart peace and your mind solidarity.
The soft grass coats itself with shy daffodils as the fields bring a feeling of freedom that feels infinite.
The cloud-grey roads pour themselves throughout the Irish countryside.
As the kindness of the sun is so sweet, she leaves homely kisses upon the ridges of my shoulders, he is the one who raises her in the dewy mornings and settles her on her knees in the cool evening breeze.
This boy was born with the sand traced below his feet - his adventure knows no limits.
He was born between the walls of the desert and found gold in its yellow speckled dust.
He is truly the most magnificent soul to walk this earth.

I've never met a man like him.
He wasn't a man of many words but at the same time he always had a mouthful to say.
Within his smile he held a reply that sparked fires within me, they would light for days.
I always adored the little things about him like how he could never go to bed before brushing his teeth or
how he hated when his feet touched the cold wooded floor in the mornings.
Or how his hand rested on my cheek every time his eyes sunk into mine.
He wasn't a man of many words, but his lips spoke volumes when on mine.
I remember the early hours of the morning when our eyes were heavy, but our hearts were full.

-I've never been more in love with life and it's all because of him.

I'm exhausted. I am tired of faces I don't know and rooms I don't feel safe in.
I'm strained by hallways of neglect and crowds of people that remind me I am small and insignificant.
I was forced to grow within walls with false security.
They never cared.
I watched my worth as a person be written on booklets that would determine my future.
Not even a name but a number in a system that gambles with my mental health.
My presence to you is nothing more than a paycheck for your time.

I'd be lying if I said I wasn't angry. I'd be lying if I said I'm not hurting or that nothing bothers me anymore, I'd be lying if I said I wasn't exhausted.
As if I wasn't wasting away in this body of mine, the body that carries me day into night, night into day, the body that has put itself through hell to keep on living.
And yet I still can't tell you why or for how much longer, but it just is that way.
-My body has a power that is beyond what this world told her she could possess.

There is a woman halfway across the world who loves him, she prepares kisses on the sleeves of his sweater on the wait of his return.
-I would wait a thousand worlds for you.

A whirlwind, the only word I could use to describe it. Spring poured itself into autumn with no remorse. I stood behind time desperately pulling it backwards.
for I knew by winter he'd be six feet under.
-the suddenness that comes with loss

All man's land

To be a woman in a world that's placed in the hands of man - is the scariest thing I have ever known.
You can be the strongest creature on earth until they claim you are weak,
Nothing will ever come of you whilst you bloom on the roots of man's land.
Normalized misogyny is the most toxic spectrum in our modern-day society it weeps upon every surface on my femininity.

The ghost of my sickness

I still remember the taste of her on my tongue.
Or the feel of her brittle hands around my throat.
I'd often scream for her to let me go but the more I did,
the more shed swallow me whole.
I keep her in a cage in my mind when everything's quiet
I hear her cry.
This memory of her is violent.
She paces around her cell bashing her head against walls,
pulling out her hair and clawing at her bones.
She was a pretty girl.
I often feel guilty about killing her.
She looked so weak with my hands around her neck, my
fingers slicing her skin.
Her face was blue, and her eyes bulged with terror.
They told me once I killed her, I'd be happy.
They told me I would feel victorious.
After her death I felt nothing.
At times I think she was a good girl with bad intentions.
When she finally passed, I felt alive
I forgot what it felt like to be starving
I felt as if I never had to be hungry again.
The water from my lungs seeped out and I caught air.
No one would warn me of the howling from her cage.
Only of success, only of the moments I wouldn't be left
feeling empty when she'd drain blood from my pours,
plucking away at my nerves.
No one would warn me of the afterlife.
For when she's not gone.
For when her ghost is my prisoner, and she haunts me for
her release.

You loved me yet you hated everything about me.
No part of me looked like her and that killed you.
-would you have still wanted me if I was more like her?

The day you see what I see

I'm so afraid.
I'm beyond petrified.
My soul can't lose you, no part of me can afford to.
My heart begins to tremble.
What if one day you wake and there, I am fast asleep, where your easy limbs lie.
You look at me as your gentle eyes start to see unfamiliar vessels beneath my skin, flaws that make my pale completion glow - yet you no longer see warmth.
The highlight along my crooked nose or my thin chapped lips that are no longer plush enough to seem kissable. Every curve becomes undesirable, the weight on my stomach and thighs hunch and the stretch marks are too heavy for your head to count.
You brew your coffee and beyond each grind of bean you start to consider them flaws.
Within every bitter sip, you taste my lips.
Then suddenly, for no apparent reason at all,
You no longer love me.

I've been missing a long time. It is killing me softly. Slipping in and out of this body of mine, it's a shell that no longer feels like home

Running laps around myself is exhausting, trying to catch up with my mind is impossible. A wasteland glazed in shimmering frost, the taste of nothing but a bittersweet tragedy on my tongue. I've never felt so alone. The tips of my fingers are bruised as I drag them lifelessly across the keyboard spilling my heart out to anyone who can hear, anyone who will care. I'm running out of words to describe this Groundhog Day. I'm running out of ways to plead for help. A pain that burns cities, crumbling them to ashes. The kind of pain that leaves the glass half empty and every day less full.

You're allowed to be angry. You're allowed to feel betrayed. There are so many things in life out of our control that may not be in our favor, this teaches us resilience, it teaches us grace. It teaches us to embrace what may be unfair and learn to accept it.
Move on to the better when it comes.
It will come.

.

Your hand is the softest I have ever held.
Your love is the kindest love I have ever felt.
Not a day goes by where I don't completely and utterly adore you.
I was once told that people climb mountains and swim oceans in search of a love like yours.
But here it lies, in my bare hands and beneath the quarries of my heart.
Like treasure it sleeps there.

-your love made me feel infinite.

Because he speaks to me as if I am glass, he is ever so desperately trying not to shatter.
He is soft. His soul is as gentle as his touch, his fingers never feel like knives on my skin.
He saw rhymes within my poetry and called it art.
He taught me that love is kind, he showed me what love is supposed to feel like.
He is safe and he is home.
He taught me forgiveness and resilience.
His words are honey coating the love I truly deserved.
-In case you ever wonder

There are nights that are harder than others, the pain never really subsides.
I can still feel him on the tips of my fingers and the warmth of his embrace around my heart.
I often wonder if he knew how much I loved him or if there was anything I should have done more.
I hope he knew how important he was and how much he changed my world.
It's been two months and I can barely bring myself to the foot of his grave.
On days like these I like to pretend that this isn't reality at all and just for a little while imagine him present. Imaging him walking through the door ready for me to hold him again, knowing the outcome I would never have stopped holding him.

I'm currently building strength in weakened bones.
Repairing and mending yourself is all a process.
There will be drafts of yourself that will only feel slightly familiar, but I promise you will find yourself again.
You will love yourself again.

I wish it were easier. I wish there were mornings where the rising sun does not sting my eyes or burn my head. I wish the morning sun were kinder to me.
The kind of kindness that the shadow of the pale grey clouds brings to my aching bones.
'I don't always feel like this'
is what I tell the people travelling by fresh souls that hitch the mountain tops in search of inspiration, oh, how my soul begs to be like theirs.
I often think about the days when I do not feel disgustingly heavy inside. And although those days are blurry and feel out of reach nothing is greater than my Love.
That boy is my reason to get up in the morning, and everyone has a reason.
So even though the morning sun is unkind and the only soothing my bones get is the daylight shadows, he makes it all worth it. Little moments that are my purpose on earth lie with him and yet again, everyone has a purpose.

They say to be stronger.
As if this body of mine isn't a cocoon soon to cave in.
The outcome is something I'm not entirely sure of.
-I don't know if I'm the butterfly or the carcass.

Even when the siren sounds, we still play merry go round.
- No matter how much damage you do, I still find forgiveness in my heart for you.

If you catch me, I'm tongue tied.
The pits in my stomach fall deeper and anxiety is now suddenly a language I'm fluent in.
The body I live in is apologetic, but it is weak.
It caves in under the hurt the world inflicts on its brittle bones, smashing them to smithereens.
-this body is my only home, please be kind to it.

I'm sorry you were made to grow up in a place that made you feel insignificant in every way.
-How could you ever call that a home?

I was not afraid to leave behind what we had; I feared what would become of me if I stayed. What kind of hell would I have had to live in?
-tell me how you see things now.

I promise you my pain was not poetic. It was sleepless nights and days of pretending I was stable enough to continue. I was tired from and of all the sadness.
-Please take my words as a refuge.

You were so devoted to loving him. The ground he stood on was plated gold that lit up in your eyes. You handed him your soul and asked for nothing in return. Look at you now, standing there with nothing in your grasp, still.

I walk past your urn every day holding back tears, tears that are so uncontrollable that if they were to fill a swimming pool, I would drown.

I am not sorry for the days I prioritize my mental health over being present.
It has taught me more than being present in your world ever has.

A year of healing looks beautiful on me. A year of age looks beautiful on me. A year of self-love has done me so much more justice than anyone else ever could.

Kiss these weeping wounds.
My body outcries, sobbing, begging.
He loves me no matter how risky it feels.
He has been inside this body of mine; he has tasted its honey core and caressed its salty flesh.
Loving it no matter how much it aches and trembles.
Loving it back to peace again.
-Soulmates

All I ever asked for was your understanding.
Only for your patience and tolerance.
That was so little to ask for.

I fell and will continue to fall in love with you in all the ways I never knew were possible.

From a young age, my mother always kept me hidden. She told me that this world is unkind and is not worthy of me. She would repeatedly warn me of the wolves that linger below my tower. How my hair as golden as the sun – the same hair little did I know, they would only pull and tear. My earthy green eyes are nothing but a forestry they will invite themselves to invade. They will howl and chant. Without hesitation would devour the curves on this body of mine for there is a hunger inside of them they must obey, yet whenever I questioned to why they behave this way shed shake her head and reply, 'Boys will be boys'.
-By the time he had come and gone I realized I will never have the power to differentiate between wolf and man.

I heard stories about the girls who were taken from under streetlamps by men who lurked in the moonlight shadows.
Stories of girls who were pushed and beaten, left for dead on rusted railway tracks.
But never did I imagine hearing about the girl who went for a run in the dusty afternoon sunshine and still never made it home.
I mourned for the mothers, daughters, and sisters.
And I mourned in fear for my own.

-In memory of Aisling Murphy

You were the first place I could ever call home. The first place that ever made me feel like I belonged.
-I owe you my everything

You do not look like him at all.
When I look at you, I see my safe place.
Your arms are shelter.
You taste like love and all things pure.
You are my healing.

And to be completely honest, it took *him* to make me realize what it was.
I knew how it felt to be loved so little that I loved so hard.
what a fool I feel about it all now.

He looked at me and saw sweat laced thighs and deep blue eyes.
but not my trembling limbs and knitted brows.
He touched and he salvaged.
Leaving my soul empty - my heart dried out.
I was forced to scrape up what was left of my mangled innocence and carry it home.
For my body now belonged to the streets, for unwanted hands to roam.

I fell asleep with books swarming my desk again.
Promising this time, I would do better.
There is a standard each of us must meet.
I tore my hair out and cried rivers just to be what you expected of me.
I have watched myself be swallowed by sleepless nights on top of early mornings.
Settling to only rise back into your expectation again.

My pillowcase has soaked these tears like a sponge one after the other, for days after each other.
My heart screamed and ached for the loss of my love.
How dare you take the young and innocent?
How dare you take my love from me?
-one sided conversations between me and God.

A woman who placed her dreams into the hands of her three daughters. A woman who gave her world to watch her girls live the life she always wanted.
-Mother

Seeds of grief have been planted in the bedding of my heart.
They grow no matter rain nor shine.
These seeds are ever green.

Because you are just a girl. Protecting you is all I will ever know. How could I let you wonder in a world that is not built to keep you safe?
-Future daughter

I am so difficult. It would be so much easier for you to give up. So much easier for you to walk away. There is a no man's land in this head of mine, a wire you must walk to ever dare set foot on this land. I promise you it is not intentional. I mean you no harm.
It is a war between me, myself, and I.
-why do you stay?

I will shoulder all the things you feel you cannot. Until you feel you can. I will hold the pieces you let drop behind until you are ready to sow them back together.
I will teach you how to be brave - the kind of bravery that will leave you with no fear when the tears start to stream. When sadness leaves you empty, you'll know deep down you will be okay for my reassurance has cradled you for decades.
-For the future children of mine

Love will come again. Love comes graciously. It blossoms from tattered roots and turns from unusual corners. It burns through the darkest nights and smoldered fires.
Even though it will never come easy;
After loss,
Love will come again.

The trees have sheltered the grass from what little snow is yet to fall.
I suppose the trees have sheltered me before in the same way.
They sheltered me the day you were taken from me.
I collapsed into them as they held me close.
Sheltering me from all the hurt that was to come my way.
To this day I still seek comfort from the armed leaves of the willow tree.

My heart cannot bring herself to understand it the way my brain can. My heart continues to long and beg for you. My heart cannot understand why it had to come to this. My brain refuses to tell her for she wants nothing more than to protect her from breaking all over again.
-My head and my heart

I want to laugh until my stomach is in a tangle. I want to dance until the needles pin my feet. I want to love you so loud that mountains echo your name. I want to feel your love in every way it makes me feel alive,
over and over again.

I have packed all my belongings and stacked them at the door. Every sinister memory I have left here, I do not need them anymore. I am moving on with a heavy heart, she has been hurting from the very start. I am going to walk new roads and lay on shoulders I've never cried on before. I'm going to live in places that these memories will never hear of from now on.
-These days are coming

I've watched kids my age lose themselves at the end of liquor bottles, accompanying themselves with people who hang on street corners offering them plastic bags of white saw dust in exchange for their youth. I've seen these lonely people in crowded rooms continuously searching for that feeling of purpose they have lost.

I've seen gloomy eyes paired with fake smiles, the tainted pen marks on suicide letters that sit in dusty drawers. These kids have been so chewed up by social norms they don't know how to *feel* anymore.

As an observer everything feels so permanent. Everything you see you know you can never change because you don't have the courage to. You watch it all unfold channeling every inner demon just for the sake of peace.

I have been going through changes. Passing through phases. Hurting in places they said would have healed by now. The expectation of moving on is blinding. I'm relapsing into open wounds with withering stitches. This constant back and forth is a never-ending war.
-grief can feel like such a lonely battle

You love to double cross me
And I love you
I kneel at the feet of my betrayer.
Always second guessing, always second chancing.
For blood should mean forgiveness
Right?
Forgiving you for every word you tore from my mouth and twisted
Every story you stole and made your own
Every promise you abandoned for you can never bring yourself to be anything more than a two timer.

Growing up, we were taught to always be the bigger person, that our peers are nothing more than a test of mortality. We are taught to stand above ignorance, to walk faster than greed and distance ourselves from envy.
It is okay to lose your patience with grace, letting all these things get the better of you.

They preach mental health until it is on their doorstep. Until its absences and missing assignments instead of crippling anxiety and deep depression. They want to preach mental health until they don't have the facilities to support the mentally ill. They ignore the signs until someone acts out. They don't want to acknowledge how their system let us down.

The place that was made mandatory for me never brought me happiness. It made me miserable. A broken system that filled me with despair. A place for preparing futures made me resent mine. I want you to know it is okay if you feel this way too, and you are NOT a failure. You have never FAILED in life.

I wish it was still November.
November held everything I loved and more.
New beginnings that I had no idea were short term.
November only ever had good intentions, filling me with hope and brought along Octobers kindness with him.
November tried so hard to bring me happiness, he was so bitter when January stole it from me.

Many loves will come in different shapes and forms. They may not stay for long or may leave in extremely painful ways, it is all about experiencing the uniqueness of their love. Love that makes you feel extraordinary. A love that will place the entire universe's happiness at the tip of your toes. You will burn like a star. It is the most indescribable feeling in the world.
-soulmates

Do you look at your brothers and envy them? For I could save them but couldn't save you?
-the guilt I feel for your passing

Sometimes the bravest thing you can be is vulnerable. When people learn of your hurt, they learn of your bravery.

If you told me two years ago, I had found a love that doesn't hurt or cost my every being to own, I would have said to you it was impossible to find such a fairy tale for he made love feel like a burden. But here I am experiencing true love for the very first time. The realization is a sigh of relief for my heart.

Your death still eats away at me.
Grief has a hold of my heart, squeezing its hardest every time I miss you.
From time to time, I think of all I could have done and all that I would have done if I had only known.
Nobody warns you of how permanent grief is.
You grieve for your entire life.
You will grieve for that somebody for eternity.
Nobody warns you about how consuming guilt is either.
That guilt I promise you is not permanent,
It heals with time.
I'm still healing with time

A man who carries five worlds on the ridges of his back.
A man who has worked long nights into tedious mornings.
Working a vicious system that left him with no self-benefit.
He did it all for those five tiny worlds.
He provided them with food, warmth, shelter as well as education, opportunity, possibilities, everything he himself had to sacrifice to make it all possible for us.
-Father

Progress is still progress.
There are days I'd rather be doing anything else but living.
Days when the sky comes crashing down and I forget who I am anymore. Or who I'm supposed to be.
Days where the hurt is so severe, my body aches getting out of bed in the morning,
But on those days, I'm still alive, I'm exactly who I need to be right when I need to be. And every trembling limb is still a step forward.
Be grateful for your progress.
Be kind to your progress and it'll be kind to you.

I told them that I'd write about you.
About how you wanted two loves rather than one.
That no matter how hard she tried to give you her everything, every time she pulled apart the seams of her skin to make herself bleed for you –
it was never enough for you.
I told them I wouldn't write about the pain.
The pain of never being enough for someone, the pain of losing a love that you one sided-ly worked so hard to provide for.

Comfort foods at the dining table in the kitchen of the house across the street.
Sweetened tea and toasted triangle sandwiches.
A distraction from all that was happening at home.
A temporary place to call home when my own was falling apart.

The feelings I have for this place will never change; the love I have for this home will no longer grow. It stopped growing the minute you abandoned me, the minute you left me alone.

Boiled spices in the cooker of the cottage right of the blue meadow. I see myself there. A life of dandelions and citrus fruits.
Growing a family in the presence of the Great Oaks on the windy farm.

We dust secrets under the rugs of living rooms that held boxing matches.
Splinter the tiles of kitchens that were beaten with dishes and flowerpots.
Curtain the windows that ever dared let anyone have a look in.
A look into what was really happening.
-the world we live in

I think about us and what we could have been if our love had only been kind.
If we had only learned to love kindly to one another.
I call for you in my dreams, I call for the romance we conjured in our early days.
It is so strange to see how it bubbled into evilness.
How can love become so bitter?
I go through phases of hating and missing you.
I know you do too.
It's now that I see how dangerous we were as kids in love.

The rain drizzled itself on the sun-tired grass of the echoey forest trail.
I search for you but only ever find myself searching.
I find you in the places I don't expect to, like in sunsets or the morning robin that sits on my windowsill daily.
But never in my arms or by the breakfast table as you watch me drink my morning coffee.
Only ever in the places I can't reach you.
-I will forever mourn your absence

I pity the ones who cannot love, who cannot show kindness to every soul.
The ones who go out their way to make you feel so unloved, so unwanted.
Do not take it personal, these people were bathed in bitterness from the moment they could walk.
They were never taught how to love others.
They were never taught the importance of gentleness when it comes to other people's feelings.
Pity them too, for they will never know the greatness of compassionate love.

Grow out in this body of mine, slip into these pale bounds.
Try on these one fit-shoes and see how far you can walk.
I will try to do the same.
We will never meet the line.
The line of understanding and accepting one another's feelings completely.

I don't think I was crazy for what I had done.
I think I was crazy in love.
Crazy enough to put myself on the line to protect the one I loved.
There's nothing more special than that.

I will forever resent my past heartbreaks, or so it feels like I will.
My heart can't handle it, the pain is indescribable.
I still feel so vulnerable when it comes to loving.
My frail body cannot physically maintain itself through another nuclear blast.
I was foolish to love again, a fool to trust another with my healing heart.
I live in fear of the worst
The worst of the pain

I read books about women in silk spun dresses with lovers who felt like forever.
These books never forewarned me of the fear love will give me, the brokenness, pieces of myself that I have had to leave behind - I do not have the time to reassemble them
That so much hurt will go into loving someone before they have even left you.

There will be those who will set you up for failure.
Those who intentionally lead you in the wrong direction.
Never hate them for it.
I've supported women who did not want to see the same strength in me.
The worst thing we can do is teach our girls to plot against each other.
Find forgiveness in your heart for these people.

I will write for you.
Verses upon stanzas that bleed with my desire for you.
That is all I can do.
I hope these words of ink stain you in ways that they never wash off.
My love will be permanent on you.

I let him in too easily.
He settled in making my bones a home.
He was too content to move.
He claimed his kingdom
and I - a young girl in love, were an easy target.

'Merry Christmas' I whispered as I watched through teary eyes, the lady who sleeps on the street corner.
I know she lost her husband last year and her son never calls anymore.
I always felt sorry for her on these December nights, especially tonight.

The homeless hostiles are swollen in the winter months as families beg for hotel rooms on the one night of the year, they can give their children a warm bed for the holiday.
The housing crisis is through the roof, and nothing is more upsetting than the children who wake up on this special day-still in no home of their own.

I watch the fear in their eyes, their faith whisking away with the bitter winds. The rising cost of living in Ireland is making our country feel less and less like a home for everyone.
Leaving those who have nothing without even a glimmer of hope.

Thank you!

Thank you! My name is Amy, I'm 17 years old and I'm from a small county in rural Ireland. I started writing poetry from a very young age as a creative outlet. Eventually, it became my safe heaven. For every journey I've been on, these words carried me through them all.

I want to thank the souls who inspired me to write this book. The souls who I have loved and lost, the souls I have loved and left and the souls I loved and will continue to love forever.

But I also want to thank *you* for being here, for holding my love in your hands and hearing my words. For being brave enough to acknowledge your hurt and strong enough to heal it.

I have been granted an amazing opportunity to work with Perspective Press Global as they bring me on a new journey to publishing my very first book. I'm ecstatic for the day my poetry unfolds from my hands into yours.

This book and its poetry are my savior, I hope it will be yours too.

With love always,

Amy

About the Author

Amy is a 17-year-old Irish student attending college in the small county of Lovely Leitrim in rural Ireland. This is her first poetry collection where she gathers memories of her experiences she has journeyed on from a young age.

As well as her love of writing, she has a big love for animals. Although she is compassionate about canine care, she intends to study English literature and become a teacher, sharing her love and knowledge of poetry.

Amy worked with Perspective Press Global to have her collection published in the hope of healing others, sharing stories of love and loss, heartbreak and healing, mental health and growth. Comforting readers who feel the same.

About the Publisher

Perspective Press Global is an independent publishing firm representing authors under the age of 20.

At Perspective Press Global, our mission is to inspire young aspiring authors that there is no such thing as being 'too young;' your voices deserve to be heard.

The firm was founded by Eleni Sophia as she struggled to find representation when she was a 13-year-old writer. We now have published young talent from around the globe – including, UK, Albania, Kosovo, and Ireland!

If you're interested in joining our team, please visit our submissions page at perspectivepressglobal.com and come say hello over on Instagram @PerspectivePressGlobal

My Heart and Her Eclipse

ISBN: 978-1-914275-97-5

Perspective Press Global Ltd

Printed in Great Britain
by Amazon

14814819R00059